Daily Structured Journal

A 30 Day Journey to a Better You

http://dailystructuredjournal.com

Published by Acropolis Scholars, LLC
St. Paul, Minnesota.

ISBN-13: 978-0692424025
ISBN-10: 0692424024

We thoroughly hope you enjoy your journey over these next 30 days. If there is anything we can do to help you out on your way, or if you have any questions, comments, concerns, musings, dedications, or requests, or just want to drop a line and say hi, we'd love to hear from you. Contact us anytime at **hello@dailystructuredjournal.com**.

Table of Contents

It takes more than one swallow or one day to make a summer, so too does a good life require habits developed over time.

- Aristotle

Introduction

Welcome to your journal and the start of a new you. This is your chance to achieve incredible personal growth and become more fully yourself – who you know deep down inside you were always meant to be. This journal will help you become more authentic, boost your confidence, and help you cultivate better relationships. We will accompany you through your journey over the next 30 days by providing practical steps you can take each day to develop new habits and acquire new skills.

The commitment is small and the results will be in proportion to how much you put into it, but with dedication, over time you will experience tremendous success.

This journal is designed to be used with a purpose. There is a direction in life you want to go, and this journal is structured to help you get there. Each day you will have the opportunity to set aside a brief time in the morning and in the evening to look over your day and set yourself up for success in reaching your goals.

Some people find journaling a difficult habit to acquire or keep up with, because when you just have blank pages in front of you it can be hard to think of what to write. Like so many things in life, oftentimes just getting started each day is the greatest difficulty.

That's why this journal is different. We've laid out clear and concrete prompts following logical steps for each day. Each of these steps is designed to help you grow in self-awareness, self-knowledge, and to accompany you day by day as a guide on the journey of becoming a better you.

Each morning you'll have the opportunity to start the day afresh with renewed mind and spirit and look over the day ahead to plan how to grow in your chosen virtue or skill. Each evening before bed you'll have the opportunity to review the day's successes and shortcomings, and make a firm actionable resolution for how you will improve on your successes for the next day. We'll also provide you with a daily reading to encourage and inspire you and to bring you focus and clarity at the end of each day.

You'll also have plenty of space each day to let your thoughts and reflections flow seamlessly onto the page. At the end of each week you'll have the opportunity to review the past seven days, see the progress you've made, and plan for the week ahead.

You get to decide which skills, personal strengths, or virtues you want to be working on. We've given you some suggestions below to help you get started.

❖	Authenticity	❖	Time Management
❖	Confidence	❖	Overcoming Shyness
❖	Gratitude	❖	Productivity
❖	Conquering Anxiety	❖	Overcoming Fears
❖	Public Speaking	❖	Conversation Skills
❖	Friendliness	❖	Writing Well

We hope you enjoy this journal, and more importantly we hope you use it to become something great. If you follow it faithfully, you will become a better you. If you like what you find inside, encounter any difficulties on the way, or if there is anything we can do to improve your experience, we would love to hear from you.

Tell us about your journey at **hello@dailystructuredjournal.com**.

Happiness is achieved through acquiring habits of excellence

- Aristotle

Set Your Goals

Write down your goals, short and long term, that are things you want to achieve or see as part of you living the life you desire. These pages are intended to grow with you through your journey in your journal since goals may change or become reprioritized as you grow. You may choose to include skills you want to obtain. This is for you, to be a place you can always return to as a reminder of your course and a check for your progress and maintenance, and for regaining momentum for continued growth.

My Goals Are...

_____

_____

_____

_____

_____

_____

_____

_____

_____

_____

_____

_____

_____

_____

_____

_____

_____

The Promise

I, _____, promise myself to write in my *Daily Structured Journal* each morning and evening for at least eight (8) consecutive days, starting on the _____ of _____, 20__.

I value this journal because it will help me to develop or improve my ability to _____
_____.

Because I am committed to becoming a better me, I will do the following three things to create the space and time I need each day to work in this journal and progress on my journey of personal growth and development:

1._____
_____
_____

2._____
_____
_____

3._____
_____
_____

Instructions

Each day provides you with some basic exercises to begin your day in the morning and to wrap up your day in the evening before bed.

The Morning Routine

Mindfulness: You will start each morning journal with a brief mindfulness exercise taken from those listed on the following pages. Mindfulness exercises like these have shown to greatly reduce your daily stress-load and improve your mood and cognitive functioning.

Gratitude: Once you are refreshed and recollected, you will be prompted to think about something you are grateful for that morning. This exercise will help you learn to see with eyes of gratitude. Try to vary it up as to what particular thing you focus on being grateful for each day, so that gratitude can really become a habit for you. Daily cultivating gratitude has scientifically proven benefits for your mood and relationships. Your responses tend to be more powerful when you start them out like this: "I am grateful for…"

Resolution: Each morning you will reaffirm the resolution you made the previous evening (more about that below), and renew your commitment to taking specific action today to grow and improve in concrete measurable ways. These resolutions help you be accountable to yourself and remind you at the start of each day where you want to be focused on.

Daily Goal: After reaffirming your specific resolution, you will identify the basic skill or virtue you are going to work on in various ways throughout the day. Naming this goal helps set the tone for your day into a growth mindset ready to face any challenge.

Writing Exercise: This is the place to let your thoughts and feelings flow out onto the page, and can be an amazing opportunity for self-discovery.

The Evening Routine

Mindfulness: You will begin each evening journal with the brief evening mindfulness exercise provided below in order to recollect yourself and clear your mind of all distractions at the end of the day. This will allow you to review the events of your day with clarity and calm.

Daily Reflection: In this brief exercise you will grow in self-awareness and gain insight into your inner motivations, habits, and behavior patterns. Here you have the opportunity to non-judgmentally assess where you've fallen short of your resolution and goals, and also where you've triumphed and flourished. We encourage you to have the courage to be vulnerable and authentic with yourself in this exercise so that in loving self-acceptance you can plan concrete steps to make progress in the future.

Resolution: Here you will identify and write out a specific action or set of actions you will take tomorrow to overcome the weaknesses and grow in your strengths. Making this firm commitment helps you be accountable to yourself and greatly increases the likelihood of you following through and making an impact on your personal growth. These resolutions have been found to be most helpful when written with "I will...." language rather than just short fragments or "I could..." language. Be bold. Be daring.

Quote of the Day: These quotes at the end of each day will draw your mind back to focus on the wisdom of philosophers, sages, and saints throughout the ages, and help inspire and motivate you in your journey to a better you.

The Weekly Check-In

Review: At the end of each week (every seven days) you will have the opportunity to look back over the past week and see the progress you've made and take notice of the areas still in need of growth. You may notice certain patterns or trends. This valuable step in self-knowledge is important for you to be able to focus on successful progress and measurable outcomes in your journey toward flourishing.

Gains: Here you can summarize the progress you've made in the past week.

Ongoing Struggles: After reviewing the previous week, take note of the areas or skills that seem to present an ongoing challenge to you. Make note of any patterns or trends. This is a time to make an honest appraisal of what areas need growth, rather than a time for self-criticism.

Looking Ahead: Now it's time to take a look at the seven days still before you. This exercise will help you become more proactive about meeting any possible challenges that may come up during the week, and to plan ahead of time how to skillfully overcome them.

Goals: You will have the opportunity to update your goals each week as you grow and develop on this journey of transformation. It can be helpful to make your goals concrete, specific, and actionable each week.

Planning Positive Experiences: An important dimension of cultivating the habits for authentic human flourishing is to plan positive experiences throughout the week. Here you will take a moment each week to plan something you can do to care for yourself and find relaxation and peace in the midst of daily life.

Mindfulness Exercises

A few words about practicing mindfulness:

Mindfulness exercises are good practice to calm yourself and collect yourself and bring yourself for the present moment. They offer a chance to pause and practice focusing and engaging in the moment. Remember, that mindfulness exercises are a practice, sometimes they are easier and sometimes more difficult. Also, they may not always make you feel good. The goal is awareness and attentiveness. It is ok if you feel uncomfortable either doing some of the practices or as a result of some of the practices. It is essential to self-knowledge and personal growth to push through the discomfort to become more aware of yourself and more able to attend to the moment or what you choose to attend to. It becomes an exercise to strengthen your will and self-control as well as your self-knowledge. Keep at it when it proves difficult and learn from those experiences, often the difficult times can teach us the most! You may even find it helpful to write down some of your observations after doing your mindfulness practices.

To benefit the most from these practices, it is important to not let our mind wander down paths of distractions or judgments. Often the mind calls up other thoughts or worries or events from our days that you may want to think about. Resist the urge to engage in these distractions. You can always go back to them later, but for the few moments you spend on mindfulness, bring yourself to be fully present. It will teach you how to be more present in other circumstances too. Also, a word about judgments: it is important to not judge yourself or the practice. It's ok to notice if you have judgments, but again, don't engage in a dialogue with them. You may find yourself thinking critical thoughts about your abilities or physical body or feeling anger about your circumstances that come to mind when doing some of these practices. All of these things are ok to feel, however, you will find great benefit from learning to just notice and be aware of these urges. By increasing your awareness of, rather than engaging with, the judgments you can move towards greater control of happiness and joy in your life. It can change your perspective and even you, if you allow it.

To do the exercises, set aside 2-3 minutes. Read through the exercise before you being so you know what to do. Then take your time with them. As you begin, you may need to read through the exercise as you do it. However, with practice, you will be able to remember the exercises and engage more fully by not having to read as you practice.

Morning Mindfulness Exercises

Exercise A:

Begin seated neutrally with both feet on the ground. Turn your attention to what you see. Notice what is immediately in front of you. Notice colors, shapes, textures. Try to only observe without labeling what you see, without judging. Breathe. Now turn your attention to what you hear. Listen to the world around you. Hear the sounds of your environment. If your attention wanders become aware of this and return to listening. Here too, try to listen without labeling or judging. Now smell. Notice smells. Notice without labeling and without judging. Breathe. Lastly notice touch. Become aware of the touch of the chair on your body, its texture, hardness or softness. Notice the touch of the air on your skin, your feet on the ground. Perhaps you notice the texture of your clothing on your skin or the touch of your top lip of your bottom lip, or your tongue in your mouth. Now take a deep breath in through your nose, exhale slowly through your mouth and bring your attention back to where you are at. What did you notice doing this mindfulness exercise? Did you become aware of sounds you haven't noticed before? Did you feel the pressure of the chair and the texture of clothing on your skin? Was it hard to observe without labeling and describing what you observed?

Exercise B:

Sit in neutral position with feet on the ground. Today we will do a breathing exercise. Inhale slowly through your nose to the count of five

(Inhale for one, two, three, four, five) then exhale slowly through your mouth on the count of seven (exhale for one, two, three, four, five, six, seven), making your exhalation longer than your inhalation. You may choose other counts that are more comfortable for you, perhaps three counts to inhale and five counts to exhale. Repeat as you continue to breathe. Your breaths may be normal or deep stomach breaths. You may exhale either through your nose or mouth. The goal is to practice focusing your awareness and minimizing distractibility.

Exercise C:

Sit in a neutral position with your feet on the floor. Have a timer or clock with you. Set the timer for 1 minute. Now hold your arms out straight in front of you so that your arms are parallel with the floor. Notice urges, feelings and sensations as you do this. Observe judgments you may have. After 1 minute relax your arms and spend a moment thinking about what you noticed.

Exercise D:

Start seated in a comfortable, neutral position. Put both feet flat on the ground. You may close your eyes or keep them open, do what is comfortable for you. Start by noticing your breath, without changing your breath. Notice your inhale and your exhale. Breathe as you normally do. Observe your body as you breathe. Notice what muscles move and work as you inhale and as you exhale. Continue to focus on your breath. If other thoughts come to your mind, notice them and allow them to float by. Turn your attention back to your breath. Begin now to visualize the air flowing in through your inhale rushing to fill your body with life-supporting oxygen. Watch the air flow in through your nose, through your lungs, through your body and into your blood, cleansing and bringing life and then leaving with waste and exiting through your nose or mouth. Now turn your focus to an area of your body that may be tense or sore or painful. Imagine healing, cleansing breath flowing into that area of your body, swirling around and delivering relief and cleansing to that area. Exhale, releasing tension and toxins out of your body. Watch the tension flow out and be gone.

15

Repeat this visualization breath three more times. Now, when you are ready, begin to bring your awareness back to the moment. Spend some time noticing how you feel and how your body feels. Think about what you noticed doing this mindfulness exercise.

Exercise E:

Start by standing in a relaxed, neutral position with your arms down by your side and your weight evenly distributed on both feet. Now close your eyes and continue to stand. Notice as you stand if your body sways. If you are strong, steady and able, try shifting your weight to your left foot. Attempt to balance on your left foot. Breathe. Return to center with weight on both feet. Then shift to your right foot and attempt to balance on your right foot. Return to center. Find balance in center. Scan your body for relaxation and tension. Notice what you find. Take a deep breath in and exhale slowly. Open your eyes and think about your experience with this mindfulness exercise. Were you able to focus? Did you have judgments? Did you notice different muscles engaging and tensing with different movement?

Exercise F:

Begin seated in a relaxed, neutral position with eyes open or closed as is comfortable for you. Now call to mind a place that you've been that is safe and enjoyable, or imagine a place you wish to go that has these same qualities. With as much detail as possible, picture the scene. Imagine the colors, the objects, the atmosphere. What is there? Are there other people there? If so, who is there? What are they doing? Now imagine sensations. Is it warm? Windy? Cloudy? Sunny? Feel the sensations as you imagine them, such as the warmth of the sun or the breeze of the wind. Turn your attention next to the sounds of your place. Hear the sounds. Is it loud? Is there music? Silence? Sounds of nature? Traffic noises? Now take it all in. Stay in this place for a few more moments, just being and noticing. Notice how your body feels. Focus on where you feel relaxed in your body and notice if you feel tension anywhere in your body. Notice any thoughts or emotions that may be part of this scene for you. Then take a deep breath and exhale

16

slowly. When you are ready, come back to the moment and reflect on your experience of this exercise. What did you notice?

Exercise G:

Sit in a neutral, relaxed position with both feet flat on the ground. Begin noticing your body. Feel the physical position of your body. Notice your head; is there tension in your forehead or jaw? Continue to breathe normally as you scan down through your face and neck. Notice if your muscles feel relaxed or tense. Is your head bent in any particular direction? Turn your attention to your shoulders. Notice their position, relaxation or tension. Perhaps you feel the chair against your shoulder blades. Continue to scan your back and front torso. Notice how your body feels in your chair. Scan your attention down and observe your hips and bottom, then to your thighs and calves. Lastly notice your ankles, then feet, then toes. Feel the ground holding your feet, pushing back against the pull of gravity.

As you do this, if thoughts enter your mind, notice them and return your attention to the physical sensations of your body. Do not judge your body, do not judge the sensations. If you feel pain, notice it but do not get stuck thinking about the pain. Practice being able to observe without making a judgment. Once you have finished scanning your body, return your attention to your surroundings and spend a few moments thinking about what you noticed doing the exercise. For example, did you notice your mind wandering and being distracted with thoughts or worries? Did you notice tension? Did you judge your body? Begin to notice what you tend to struggle with when practicing mindfulness.

Evening Mindfulness Exercise

Evening Exercise:

Sit in neutral position with feet flat on the floor in front of you, eyes open or closed. Take a deep breath in and slowly exhale. Turn your attention to your thoughts. Notice any thoughts you are having or if you aren't having any — if your mind is blank. Try to just observe your thoughts like leaves floating down a stream. Don't pick up the leaves, just watch and be aware of them. Continue to breathe. Now bring your awareness to your emotions. Notice your emotions. Do not judge them nor try to change them in this moment. Only be aware of what you are feeling. Lastly bring your awareness to sensations. Notice textures, temperature, pressure; feel your physical body in its space. Now return to your breathing. Take a deep breath in and slowly release it. Bring your attention back to the moment. What did you notice doing this exercise?

Alternate Mindfulness Exercises

*Bonus Alternate Exercise 1:

Begin seated in a relaxed, neutral position with your feet on the ground and your eyes open or closed. Turn your attention to your emotions. Notice what you are feeling, your mood, attitude, perspective. Remember to just observe. Don't judge your emotions nor try to change them, just be aware of them. Now call to mind a person whom you love and cherish, someone you care about. This person may be someone you know or a character in a story. Picture this person in your mind. See their face and unique features. Hear them, the sound of their voice as you know it or imagine it. Listen to their laugh in your mind. Bring to mind any smells that you associate with this person. Call to mind sensations associated with this person. Spend some time just being with this person in your mind. Now bring your attention to your emotions. Notice how you feel, your mood, attitudes, and perspective. Then, when you are ready, come back to the moment. Reflect on your experience with this exercise. What did you notice? Did your emotions change, if so, how? Did you notice distractions? Judgments?

*Bonus Alternate Exercise 2 (Long Form):

This mindfulness exercise is a short practice of progressive muscle relaxation. Start with a deep stomach breath, inhaling through your mouth slowly for three counts, hold your breath for two counts, then exhale slowly for three counts through your mouth. Repeat. Now begin with your face. Squish your face up tight, as though you are puckering from tasting something super sour. Hold this for a count of five. Notice the tension building, then inhale and exhale slowly as you release the tension and relax for a count of seven. Feel the tension melt away and drip off your nose and chin as you relax. Then re-engage your facial tension and hold for five, notice the tension and feeling hard muscles, and exhale as you release all the tension and worry and frustration for a count of seven.

Now move to your jaw. Open your mouth as wide and open as you can to feel tension in your jaw and lips of your mouth, hold for five, then release and relax your jaw, allowing it to close to a slightly open, lips slightly parted, relaxed position. Feel the tension melt. Notice your muscles feeling softer and lighter. Then re-engage the tension in your jaw, letting it build and feel how hard the muscles are. Count to five and exhale as you release all that tension with your breath. Allow your jaw to relax into a neutral, slightly open position. Take a deep breath in, hold for a moment, and then exhale slowly.

Now focus on your shoulders. Tense your shoulders by lifting them up, up, up to your ears. Feel the muscles hard and tight. Feel the tension holding your shoulders. Now exhale and release. Your muscles are soft, yet strong, supple and relaxed. Now re-engage the tension in your shoulders feel them getting harder and tighter, all the tension and frustrations of the day concentrating in your shoulders. Then exhale and feel the tension and frustrations wash away down the shoulder blades and out of you. Your muscles are softer and more supple now. Now push or pull your shoulders down as far you can, trying to push your shoulder blades into your hips. Feel the tension building, count to five increasing it with every count, and then release and relax, allow your shoulders to float up to their natural position, more relaxed than when you started. Remember as you tense and relax different muscle groups to keep tension from creeping into muscles that you previously relaxed. Tense only the muscles specified and keep the rest of your body as relaxed as possible. Take a deep breath in and exhale slowly.

Turn your attention to your hands and squeeze them into a fist as tight as you can. Squeeze hard and hold, making a tighter fist with every count up to five. Then relax. The tension rushes away and drips down your fingers and is gone. Your hands hang limp in a relaxed, natural open position. Count to seven as you breathe and feel your hands ever more relaxed. Then re-engage the tension and fists. Hold the tension for a count of five, noticing the tension and how it feels in your hands. Now relax your hands. Notice how they might feel so light that they almost feel as though they are floating.

Now squeeze your buttocks and gluteal muscles as tight as you can. Build the tension in your pelvis and hip area. Squeeze tight, making it hard. Then relax and feel the tension melt away. Feel relaxed for a count of seven then re-engage for five and relax for seven. Now squeeze your legs together to build tension in your legs. Hold, hold, hold that tension, hard and tense. Hold for five then exhale and relax for seven. Feel the soft and supple relaxation in your legs. Re-engage for five and relax for seven.

Lastly turn your attention to your ankles and feet. Flex your feet building tension in your feet, ankles, and legs. Hold for five. The relax, allowing your feet to rest in a neutral positon. Then point your feet as hard as you can. Point and hold. Tension builds in your toes, feet, ankles and legs. Hold for five and exhale as your relax, allowing the tension to flow down your legs, down your ankles and run right off your toes and away. Feel the relaxation. Now take a moment to scan your body and notice how it feels. Notice if some areas feel relaxed, and if some still hold some tension. Allow yourself to rest in this relaxation for a moment. Then take a deep stomach breath in to the count of three, hold for two, and then exhale slowly to the count of three or four. Take a moment to reflect on what you noticed doing this exercise.

The Journal

<u>Morning</u>

1. Mindfulness Exercise

Take a few moments to go through one of the brief mindfulness exercises provided at the beginning of the Journal. Today follow Morning Exercise A.

2. Gratitude

List one thing you are grateful for today.

_____

_____

_____

3. Resolution: Write down one thing you can do today to help you begin your journey towards growth and accomplish your goal for the week.

_____

_____

_____

4. Daily Goal

Write down a practice or skill that can help you work toward your resolution today?

_____

_____

_____

5. Writing Exercise

Write for two minutes on anything.

_____

_____

_____

_____

_____

Evening

1. Mindfulness Exercise

Take a moment to go through the brief evening mindfulness exercise provided at the beginning of the Journal.

2. Reflect on Your Day

What went well today? How did you develop or improve (even in small ways) on the specific virtue or skill you're working on this week?

_____

_____

_____

What one or two things do you think need further work in order to develop this virtue or skill?

_____

_____

_____

What specific situations or circumstances are these shortcomings related to?

_____

_____

_____

3. Resolution
Write down what you're going to work on tomorrow to continue to develop your specific skill or virtue for this week. Consider doing something that specifically relates to overcoming the challenge you experienced today.

_____

_____

_____

_____

Quote of the Day:

"What is a compassionate heart? It is a heart on fire for the whole of creation, for humanity, for the birds, for the animals, for demons, and for all that exists... By the strong and vehement mercy that grips such a person's heart, and by such great compassion, the heart is humbled and one cannot bear to hear or to see any injury or slight sorrow in anything in creation. For this reason, such a person offers up tearful prayer continually even for irrational beasts, for the enemies of the truth, and for those who harm her or him, that they be protected and receive mercy, because of the great compassion that burns without measure in a heart that is in the likeness of God."
— Isaac of Nineveh

*Week 1 (Day 2), Date: __/__/20_*

<u>Morning</u>

1. Mindfulness Exercise

Take a few moments to go through one of the brief mindfulness exercises provided at the beginning of the Journal. Today follow Morning Exercise B.

2. Gratitude

List one thing you are grateful for today. Think of something new from yesterday.

_____

_____

_____

3. Reaffirm your resolution from last night's journal. Write it here.

_____

_____

_____

4. Daily Goal

Write down a practical skill that can help you work toward your resolution today.

_____

_____

_____

5. Writing Exercise

Write for two minutes on anything.

_____

_____

_____

_____

_____

_____

Evening

1. Mindfulness Exercise

Take a moment to go through the brief evening mindfulness exercise provided at the beginning of the Journal.

2. Reflect on Your Day

What went well today? How did you develop or improve (even in small ways) on the specific virtue or skill you're working on this week?

_____
_____
_____

What one or two things do you think need further work in order to develop this virtue or skill?

_____
_____
_____

What specific situations or circumstances are these short coming related to?

_____
_____
_____

3. Resolution
Write down what you're going to work on tomorrow to continue to develop your specific skill or virtue for this week. Consider doing something that specifically relates to overcoming the challenges you experienced today

_____
_____
_____
_____
_____
_____

Quote of the Day:

"Those who say that we should love our fellow-citizens but not foreigners, destroy the universal brotherhood of mankind, with which benevolence and justice would perish forever."
— Marcus Tullius Cicero

Morning

1. Mindfulness Exercise

Take a few moments to go through one of the brief mindfulness exercises provided at the beginning of the Journal. Today follow Morning Exercise C.

2. Gratitude

List one thing you are grateful for today. Think of something new from yesterday.

_____

_____

_____

3. Reaffirm your resolution from last night's journal. Write it here.

_____

_____

_____

4. Daily Goal

Write down a practical skill that can help you work toward your resolution today.

_____

_____

_____

5. Writing Exercise

Write for two minutes on anything.

_____

_____

_____

_____

_____

_____

Week 1 (Day 3), Date: __/__/20__

<u>Evening</u>

1. Mindfulness Exercise

Take a moment to go through the brief evening mindfulness exercise provided at the beginning of the Journal.

2. Reflect on Your Day

What went well today? How did you develop or improve (even in small ways) on the specific virtue or skill you're working on this week?

_____
_____
_____

What one or two things do you think need further work in order to develop this virtue or skill?

_____
_____
_____

What specific situations/circumstances are these shortcomings related to?

_____
_____
_____

3. Resolution

Write down what you're going to work on tomorrow to continue to develop your specific skill for this week. Consider doing something that specifically relates to overcoming the challenges you experienced today.

_____
_____
_____
_____
_____
_____

Quote of the Day:

"Abba Anthony said, 'Whoever hammers a lump of iron, first decides what he is going to make of it, a scythe, a sword, or an axe. Even so we ought to make up our minds what kind of virtue we want to forge or we labor in vain.'"
— The Sayings of the Desert Abbas

Morning

1. Mindfulness Exercise

Take a few moments to go through one of the brief mindfulness exercises provided at the beginning of the Journal. Today follow Morning Exercise D.

2. Gratitude

List one thing you are grateful for today. Think of something new from yesterday.

_____

_____

_____

3. Reaffirm your resolution from last night's journal. Write it here.

_____

_____

_____

4. Daily Goal

Write down a practical skill that can help you work toward your resolution today

_____

_____

_____

5. Writing Exercise

Write for two minutes on anything.

_____

_____

_____

_____

_____

_____

<u>Evening</u>

1. Mindfulness Exercise

Take a moment to go through the brief evening mindfulness exercise provided at the beginning of the Journal.

2. Reflect on Your Day

What went well today? How did you develop or improve (even in small ways) on the specific virtue or skill you're working on this week?

_____

_____

_____

What one or two things do you think need further work in order to develop this virtue or skill?

_____

_____

_____

What specific situations/circumstances are these shortcomings related to?

_____

_____

_____

3. Resolution

Write down what you're going to work on tomorrow to continue to develop your specific skill for this week. Consider doing something that specifically relates to overcoming the challenges you experienced today.

_____

_____

_____

_____

_____

_____

Quote of the Day:

"How much time he gains who does not look to see what his neighbor says or does or thinks, but only at what he does himself, and makes it just and holy."
— Marcus Aurelius

Morning

1. Mindfulness Exercise

Take a few moments to go through one of the brief mindfulness exercises provided at the beginning of the Journal. Today follow Morning Exercise E.

2. Gratitude

List one thing you are grateful for today. Think of something new from yesterday.

_____

_____

_____

3. Reaffirm your resolution from last night's journal. Write it here.

_____

_____

_____

4. Daily Goal

Write down a practical skill that can help you work toward your resolution today.

_____

_____

_____

5. Writing Exercise

Write for two minutes on anything.

_____

_____

_____

_____

_____

_____

<u>Evening</u>

1. Mindfulness Exercise

Take a moment to go through the brief evening mindfulness exercise provided at the beginning of the Journal.

2. Reflect on Your Day

What went well today? How did you develop or improve (even in small ways) on the specific virtue or skill you're working on this week?

_____
_____
_____

What one or two things do you think need further work in order to develop this virtue or skill?

_____
_____
_____

What specific situations/circumstances are these shortcomings related to?

_____
_____
_____

3. Resolution
Write down what you're going to work on tomorrow to continue to develop your specific skill for this week. Consider doing something that specifically relates to overcoming the challenges you experienced today.

_____
_____
_____
_____
_____
_____
_____

Quote of the Day:

"A tree is known by its fruit; a person by their deeds. A good deed is never lost; the one who sows courtesy reaps friendship, and the one who plants kindness gathers love."
— Basil the Great

Morning

1. Mindfulness Exercise

Take a few moments to go through one of the brief mindfulness exercises provided at the beginning of the Journal. Today follow Morning Exercise F.

2. Gratitude

List one thing you are grateful for today. Think of something new from yesterday.

_____

_____

_____

3. Reaffirm your resolution from last night's journal. Write it here.

_____

_____

_____

4. Daily Goal

Write down a practical skill that can help you work toward your resolution today.

_____

_____

_____

5. Writing Exercise

Write for two minutes on anything.

_____

_____

_____

_____

_____

_____

Evening

1. Mindfulness Exercise

Take a moment to go through the brief evening mindfulness exercise provided at the beginning of the Journal.

2. Reflect on Your Day

What went well today? How did you develop or improve (even in small ways) on the specific virtue or skill you're working on this week?

_____
_____
_____

What one or two things do you think need further work in order to develop this virtue or skill?

_____
_____
_____

What specific situations/circumstances are these shortcomings related to?

_____
_____
_____

3. Resolution

Write down what you're going to work on tomorrow to continue to develop your specific skill for this week. Consider doing something that specifically relates to overcoming the challenges you experienced today.

_____
_____
_____
_____
_____
_____

Quote of the Day:

"A person's best friend is the one who not only desires the good for him or her but desires it for the friend's own sake (even though nobody might ever know it): and this condition is best fulfilled by his attitude towards himself – and similarly with all the other attributes that go to define a friend."
— Aristotle

Morning

1. Mindfulness Exercise

Take a few moments to go through one of the brief mindfulness exercises provided at the beginning of the Journal. Today follow Morning Exercise G.

2. Gratitude

List one thing you are grateful for today. Think of something new from yesterday.

_____

_____

_____

3. Reaffirm your resolution from last night's journal. Write it here.

_____

_____

_____

4. Daily Goal

Write down a practical skill that can help you work toward your resolution today.

_____

_____

_____

5. Writing Exercise

Write for two minutes on anything.

_____

_____

_____

_____

_____

_____

Evening

1. Mindfulness Exercise

Take a moment to go through the brief evening mindfulness exercise provided at the beginning of the Journal.

2. Reflect on Your Day

What went well today? How did you develop or improve (even in small ways) on the specific virtue or skill you're working on this week?

_____

_____

_____

What one or two things do you think need further work in order to develop this virtue or skill?

_____

_____

_____

What specific situations/circumstances are these shortcomings related to?

_____

_____

_____

3. Resolution

Write down what you're going to work on tomorrow to continue to develop your specific skill for this week. Consider doing something that specifically relates to overcoming the challenges you experienced today.

_____

_____

_____

_____

_____

_____

Quote of the Day:

"When you arise in the morning, think of what a precious privilege it is to be alive – to breathe, to think, to enjoy, to love."
— Marcus Aurelius

<u>Weekly Check-In</u>

1. Review

Take a moment to reflect on the past week, looking over your notes, and noticing any patterns or trends.

2. Gains

Look at the progress you've made toward your goal over the past week. Write a short summary of your progress here.

_____

_____

_____

_____

_____

_____

_____

3. Ongoing Struggles

Summarize the areas in need of continued growth, and identify the skill or virtue necessary to succeed. Write a brief summary here.

_____

_____

_____

_____

_____

_____

_____

4. Looking Ahead

Give yourself a moment to look over the next seven days. Are there any particular challenges or unique circumstances that you foresee might need special attention? What concrete steps can you plan to take in order to handle these events as best you can? Write these here.

_____

_____

_____

_____

_____

5. Goals

Set a concrete, actionable goal for improving this week. Write your goal here.

_____

_____

_____

_____

_____

6. Planning Positive Experiences

What is one thing you can do to care for yourself this week?

_____

_____

_____

_____

_____

Week 2 (Day 8), Date: __/__/20__

<u>Morning</u>

1. Mindfulness Exercise

Take a few moments to go through one of the brief mindfulness exercises provided at the beginning of the Journal. Today follow Morning Exercise A.

2. Gratitude

List one thing you are grateful for today. Think of something new from yesterday.

_____
_____
_____

3. Reaffirm your resolution from last night's journal. Write it here.

_____
_____
_____

4. Daily Goal

Write down a practical skill that can help you work toward your resolution today.

_____
_____
_____

5. Writing Exercise

Write for two minutes on anything.

_____
_____
_____
_____
_____
_____

Evening

1. Mindfulness Exercise

Take a moment to go through the brief evening mindfulness exercise provided at the beginning of the Journal.

2. Reflect on Your Day

What went well today? How did you develop or improve (even in small ways) on the specific virtue or skill you're working on this week?

_____

_____

_____

What one or two things do you think need further work in order to develop this virtue or skill?

_____

_____

_____

What specific situations/circumstances are these shortcomings related to?

_____

_____

_____

3. Resolution
Write down what you're going to work on tomorrow to continue to develop your specific skill for this week. Consider doing something that specifically relates to overcoming the challenges you experienced today.

_____

_____

_____

_____

_____

_____

Quote of the Day:

"The happiness of your life depends upon the quality of your thoughts: therefore, guard accordingly, and take care that you entertain no notions unsuitable to virtue and reasonable nature."
— Marcus Aurelius

<u>Morning</u>

1. Mindfulness Exercise

Take a few moments to go through one of the brief mindfulness exercises provided at the beginning of the Journal. Today follow Morning Exercise B.

2. Gratitude

List one thing you are grateful for today. Think of something new from yesterday.

_____

_____

_____

3. Reaffirm your resolution from last night's journal. Write it here.

_____

_____

_____

4. Daily Goal

Write down a practical skill that can help you work toward your resolution today.

_____

_____

_____

5. Writing Exercise

Write for two minutes on anything.

_____

_____

_____

_____

_____

_____

Evening

1. Mindfulness Exercise

Take a moment to go through the brief evening mindfulness exercise provided at the beginning of the Journal.

2. Reflect on Your Day

What went well today? How did you develop or improve (even in small ways) on the specific virtue or skill you're working on this week?

_____

_____

_____

What one or two things do you think need further work in order to develop this virtue or skill?

_____

_____

_____

What specific situations/circumstances are these shortcomings related to?

_____

_____

_____

3. Resolution

Write down what you're going to work on tomorrow to continue to develop your specific skill for this week. Consider doing something that specifically relates to overcoming the challenges you experienced today.

_____

_____

_____

_____

_____

_____

Quote of the Day:

"True happiness is the meaning and the purpose of life, the whole aim and end of human existence."
— Aristotle

_____
_____
_____
_____
_____
_____
_____
_____
_____
_____
_____
_____
_____
_____
_____
_____
_____
_____
_____
_____
_____
_____
_____
_____
_____
_____
_____
_____
_____

Morning

1. Mindfulness Exercise

Take a few moments to go through one of the brief mindfulness exercises provided at the beginning of the Journal. Today follow Morning Exercise C.

2. Gratitude

List one thing you are grateful for today. Think of something new from yesterday.

_____

_____

_____

3. Reaffirm your resolution from last night's journal. Write it here.

_____

_____

_____

4. Daily Goal

Write down a practical skill that can help you work toward your resolution today.

_____

_____

_____

5. Writing Exercise

Write for two minutes on anything.

_____

_____

_____

_____

_____

_____

<u>Evening</u>

1. Mindfulness Exercise

Take a moment to go through the brief evening mindfulness exercise provided at the beginning of the Journal.

2. Reflect on Your Day

What went well today? How did you develop or improve (even in small ways) on the specific virtue or skill you're working on this week?

_____

_____

_____

What one or two things do you think need further work in order to develop this virtue or skill?

_____

_____

_____

What specific situations/circumstances are these shortcomings related to?

_____

_____

_____

3. Resolution

Write down what you're going to work on tomorrow to continue to develop your specific skill for this week. Consider doing something that specifically relates to overcoming the challenges you experienced today.

_____

_____

_____

_____

_____

_____

Quote of the Day:

"True happiness is to enjoy the present, without anxious dependence upon the future, not to amuse ourselves with either hopes or fears but to rest satisfied with what we have, which is sufficient, for he that is so wants nothing. The greatest blessings of mankind are within us and within our reach. A wise man is content with his lot, whatever it may be, without wishing for what he has not."
— Seneca

Way to Go! Keep up the great work!

Let's check in! You have been journaling in your journal perhaps a few days or maybe for many, many weeks. Either way it is good to check in with yourself to keep on track. Journaling consistently morning and evening is a surprisingly challenging commitment, even when the reward of personal growth is felt. Perhaps it's the process of being vulnerable, the change in routine, or the uncertainty or even fear of obtaining personal growth. Take a moment now to think about what, if anything, is getting in your way of daily journaling and how to overcome these roadblocks. If journaling is going well, take a moment to write down what is working and what keeps you on track.

_____

_____

_____

_____

_____

_____

_____

_____

_____

_____

_____

_____

_____

_____

_____

_____

_____

_____

_____

_____

Taking the time to do your journal can help you achieve and maintain personal growth and development. However, you must be willing to risk learning more about yourself and perhaps even feeling uncomfortable as you make changes. This is important to remember; change can be uncomfortable because it is unfamiliar and takes time to become part of a habit. It requires acceptance and willingness. If you are struggling with motivation and making changes, are there areas of yourself that you need to accept and work on willingness to change? If so, how are you going to choose acceptance and willingness?

_____

_____

_____

_____

_____

_____

_____

_____

_____

_____

_____

_____

_____

_____

_____

_____

_____

A Final Note: These questions may be tough to answer. The goal is to provide space to show compassion to yourself if you are struggling and also to encourage you to find ways to push through the challenges as you keep on the path you started so you can reach your goals. Keep it up!

Morning

1. Mindfulness Exercise

Take a few moments to go through one of the brief mindfulness exercises provided at the beginning of the Journal. Today follow Morning Exercise D.

2. Gratitude

List one thing you are grateful for today. Think of something new from yesterday.

_____

_____

_____

3. Reaffirm your resolution from last night's journal. Write it here.

_____

_____

_____

4. Daily Goal

Write down a practical skill that can help you work toward your resolution today.

_____

_____

_____

5. Writing Exercise

Write for two minutes on anything.

_____

_____

_____

_____

_____

_____

Evening

1. Mindfulness Exercise

Take a moment to go through the brief evening mindfulness exercise provided at the beginning of the Journal.

2. Reflect on Your Day

What went well today? How did you develop or improve (even in small ways) on the specific virtue or skill you're working on this week?

_____
_____
_____

What one or two things do you think need further work in order to develop this virtue or skill?

_____
_____
_____

What specific situations/circumstances are these shortcomings related to?

_____
_____
_____

3. Resolution

Write down what you're going to work on tomorrow to continue to develop your specific skill for this week. Consider doing something that specifically relates to overcoming the challenges you experienced today.

_____
_____
_____
_____
_____
_____

Quote of the Day:

"You have power over your mind – not outside events. Realize this, and you will find strength."
— Marcus Aurelius

Morning

1. Mindfulness Exercise

Take a few moments to go through one of the brief mindfulness exercises provided at the beginning of the Journal. Today follow Morning Exercise E.

2. Gratitude

List one thing you are grateful for today. Think of something new from yesterday.

_____

_____

_____

3. Reaffirm your resolution from last night's journal. Write it here.

_____

_____

_____

4. Daily Goal

Write down a practical skill that can help you work toward your resolution today.

_____

_____

_____

5. Writing Exercise

Write for two minutes on anything.

_____

_____

_____

_____

_____

_____

Week 2 (Day 12), Date: __/__/20__

Evening

1. Mindfulness Exercise

Take a moment to go through the brief evening mindfulness exercise provided at the beginning of the Journal.

2. Reflect on Your Day

What went well today? How did you develop or improve (even in small ways) on the specific virtue or skill you're working on this week?

_____

_____

_____

What one or two things do you think need further work in order to develop this virtue or skill?

_____

_____

_____

What specific situations/circumstances are these shortcomings related to?

_____

_____

_____

3. Resolution

Write down what you're going to work on tomorrow to continue to develop your specific skill for this week. Consider doing something that specifically relates to overcoming the challenges you experienced today.

_____

_____

_____

_____

_____

_____

Quote of the Day:

"Waste no more time arguing about what a good person should be. Be one."

— Marcus Aurelius

Week 2 (Day 13), Date: __/__/20__

<u>Morning</u>

1. Mindfulness Exercise

Take a few moments to go through one of the brief mindfulness exercises provided at the beginning of the Journal. Today follow Morning Exercise F.

2. Gratitude

List one thing you are grateful for today. Think of something new from yesterday.

_____

_____

_____

3. Reaffirm your resolution from last night's journal. Write it here.

_____

_____

_____

4. Daily Goal

Write down a practical skill that can help you work toward your resolution today.

_____

_____

_____

5. Writing Exercise

Write for two minutes on anything.

_____

_____

_____

_____

_____

_____

Week 2 (Day 13), Date: __/__/20__

Evening

1. Mindfulness Exercise

Take a moment to go through the brief evening mindfulness exercise provided at the beginning of the Journal.

2. Reflect on Your Day

What went well today? How did you develop or improve (even in small ways) on the specific virtue or skill you're working on this week?

_____
_____
_____

What one or two things do you think need further work in order to develop this virtue or skill?

_____
_____
_____

What specific situations/circumstances are these shortcomings related to?

_____
_____
_____

3. Resolution

Write down what you're going to work on tomorrow to continue to develop your specific skill for this week. Consider doing something that specifically relates to overcoming the challenges you experienced today.

_____
_____
_____
_____
_____
_____

Quote of the Day:

"What is morally wrong can never be advantageous, even when it enables you to make some gain that you believe to be to your advantage. The mere act of believing that some wrongful course of action constitutes an advantage is pernicious."
— Marcus Tullius Cicero

Morning

1. Mindfulness Exercise

Take a few moments to go through one of the brief mindfulness exercises provided at the beginning of the Journal. Today follow Morning Exercise G.

2. Gratitude

List one thing you are grateful for today. Think of something new from yesterday.

_____

_____

_____

3. Reaffirm your resolution from last night's journal. Write it here.

_____

_____

_____

4. Daily Goal

Write down a practical skill that can help you work toward your resolution today.

_____

_____

_____

5. Writing Exercise

Write for two minutes on anything.

_____

_____

_____

_____

_____

_____

<u>Evening</u>

1. Mindfulness Exercise

Take a moment to go through the brief evening mindfulness exercise provided at the beginning of the Journal.

2. Reflect on Your Day

What went well today? How did you develop or improve (even in small ways) on the specific virtue or skill you're working on this week?

_____

_____

_____

What one or two things do you think need further work in order to develop this virtue or skill?

_____

_____

_____

What specific situations/circumstances are these shortcomings related to?

_____

_____

_____

3. Resolution

Write down what you're going to work on tomorrow to continue to develop your specific skill for this week. Consider doing something that specifically relates to overcoming the challenges you experienced today.

_____

_____

_____

_____

_____

_____

Quote of the Day:

"We must not say every mistake is a foolish one."
— Marcus Tullius Cicero

<u>Weekly Check-In</u>

1. Review

Take a moment to reflect on the past week, looking over your notes, and noticing any patterns or trends.

2. Gains

Look at the progress you've made toward your goal over the past week. Write a short summary of your progress here.

_____
_____
_____
_____
_____
_____
_____

3. Ongoing Struggles

Summarize the areas in need of continued growth, and identify the skill or virtue necessary to succeed. Write a brief summary here.

_____
_____
_____
_____
_____
_____
_____

4. Looking Ahead

Give yourself a moment to look over the next seven days. Are there any particular challenges or unique circumstances that you foresee might need special attention? What concrete steps can you plan to take in order to handle these events as best you can? Write these here.

_____

_____

_____

_____

_____

5. Goals

Set a concrete, actionable goal for improving this week. Write your goal here.

_____

_____

_____

_____

_____

6. Planning Positive Experiences

What is one thing you can do to care for yourself this week?

_____

_____

_____

_____

_____

Morning

1. Mindfulness Exercise

Take a few moments to go through one of the brief mindfulness exercises provided at the beginning of the Journal. Today follow Morning Exercise A.

2. Gratitude

List one thing you are grateful for today. Think of something new from yesterday.

_____

_____

_____

3. Reaffirm your resolution from last night's journal. Write it here.

_____

_____

_____

4. Daily Goal

Write down a practical skill that can help you work toward your resolution today.

_____

_____

_____

5. Writing Exercise

Write for two minutes on anything.

_____

_____

_____

_____

_____

_____

Week 3 (Day 15), Date: __/__/20__

<u>Evening</u>

1. Mindfulness Exercise

Take a moment to go through the brief evening mindfulness exercise provided at the beginning of the Journal.

2. Reflect on Your Day

What went well today? How did you develop or improve (even in small ways) on the specific virtue or skill you're working on this week?

_____

_____

_____

What one or two things do you think need further work in order to develop this virtue or skill?

_____

_____

_____

What specific situations/circumstances are these shortcomings related to?

_____

_____

_____

3. Resolution

Write down what you're going to work on tomorrow to continue to develop your specific skill for this week. Consider doing something that specifically relates to overcoming the challenges you experienced today.

_____

_____

_____

_____

_____

_____

Quote of the Day:

"The first stage of true tranquility consists in silencing the lips when the heart is excited. The second, in silencing the mind when the soul is still excited. The goal is a perfect peacefulness even in the middle of the raging storm."
— John Climacus

Way to Go! Keep up the great work!

Let's check in! You have been journaling in your journal perhaps a few days or maybe for many, many weeks. Either way it is good to check in with yourself to keep on track. Journaling consistently morning and evening is a surprisingly challenging commitment, even when the reward of personal growth is felt. Perhaps it's the process of being vulnerable, the change in routine, or the uncertainty or even fear of obtaining personal growth. Take a moment now to think about what, if anything, is getting in your way of daily journaling and how to overcome these roadblocks. If journaling is going well, take a moment to write down what is working and what keeps you on track.

Taking the time to do your journal can help you achieve and maintain personal growth and development. However, you must be willing to risk learning more about yourself and perhaps even feeling uncomfortable as you make changes. This is important to remember; change can be uncomfortable because it is unfamiliar and takes time to become part of a habit. It requires acceptance and willingness. If you are struggling with motivation and making changes, are there areas of yourself that you need to accept and work on willingness to change? If so, how are you going to choose acceptance and willingness?

A Final Note: These questions may be tough to answer. The goal is to provide space to show compassion to yourself if you are struggling and also to encourage you to find ways to push through the challenges as you keep on the path you started so you can reach your goals. Keep it up!

Morning

1. Mindfulness Exercise

Take a few moments to go through one of the brief mindfulness exercises provided at the beginning of the Journal. Today follow Morning Exercise B.

2. Gratitude

List one thing you are grateful for today. Think of something new from yesterday.

_____
_____
_____

3. Reaffirm your resolution from last night's journal. Write it here.

_____
_____
_____

4. Daily Goal

Write down a practical skill that can help you work toward your resolution today.

_____
_____
_____

5. Writing Exercise

Write for two minutes on anything.

_____
_____
_____
_____
_____
_____

<u>Evening</u>

1. Mindfulness Exercise

Take a moment to go through the brief evening mindfulness exercise provided at the beginning of the Journal.

2. Reflect on Your Day

What went well today? How did you develop or improve (even in small ways) on the specific virtue or skill you're working on this week?

_____

_____

_____

What one or two things do you think need further work in order to develop this virtue or skill?

_____

_____

_____

What specific situations/circumstances are these shortcomings related to?

_____

_____

_____

3. Resolution

Write down what you're going to work on tomorrow to continue to develop your specific skill for this week. Consider doing something that specifically relates to overcoming the challenges you experienced today.

_____

_____

_____

_____

_____

_____

Quote of the Day:

"Day by day, what you choose, what you think and what you do is who you become."
— Heraclitus

Morning

1. Mindfulness Exercise

Take a few moments to go through one of the brief mindfulness exercises provided at the beginning of the Journal. Today follow Morning Exercise C.

2. Gratitude

List one thing you are grateful for today. Think of something new from yesterday.

_____

_____

_____

3. Reaffirm your resolution from last night's journal. Write it here.

_____

_____

_____

4. Daily Goal

Write down a practical skill that can help you work toward your resolution today.

_____

_____

_____

5. Writing Exercise

Write for two minutes on anything.

_____

_____

_____

_____

_____

_____

Evening

1. Mindfulness Exercise

Take a moment to go through the brief evening mindfulness exercise provided at the beginning of the Journal.

2. Reflect on Your Day

What went well today? How did you develop or improve (even in small ways) on the specific virtue or skill you're working on this week?

_____

_____

_____

What one or two things do you think need further work in order to develop this virtue or skill?

_____

_____

_____

What specific situations/circumstances are these shortcomings related to?

_____

_____

_____

3. Resolution

Write down what you're going to work on tomorrow to continue to develop your specific skill for this week. Consider doing something that specifically relates to overcoming the challenges you experienced today.

_____

_____

_____

_____

_____

_____

Quote of the Day:

"I count him braver who overcomes his desires than him who conquers his enemies, for the hardest victory is over the self."

— Aristotle

Morning

1. Mindfulness Exercise

Take a few moments to go through one of the brief mindfulness exercises provided at the beginning of the Journal. Today follow Morning Exercise D.

2. Gratitude

List one thing you are grateful for today. Think of something new from yesterday.

_____

_____

_____

3. Reaffirm your resolution from last night's journal. Write it here.

_____

_____

_____

4. Daily Goal

Write down a practical skill that can help you work toward your resolution today.

_____

_____

_____

5. Writing Exercise

Write for two minutes on anything.

_____

_____

_____

_____

_____

_____

<u>Evening</u>

1. Mindfulness Exercise

Take a moment to go through the brief evening mindfulness exercise provided at the beginning of the Journal.

2. Reflect on Your Day

What went well today? How did you develop or improve (even in small ways) on the specific virtue or skill you're working on this week?

_____

_____

_____

What one or two things do you think need further work in order to develop this virtue or skill?

_____

_____

_____

What specific situations/circumstances are these shortcomings related to?

_____

_____

_____

3. Resolution

Write down what you're going to work on tomorrow to continue to develop your specific skill for this week. Consider doing something that specifically relates to overcoming the challenges you experienced today.

_____

_____

_____

_____

_____

_____

Quote of the Day:

"Anger is an acid that can do more harm to the vessel in which it is stored than to anything on which it is poured."

— Seneca

_____
_____
_____
_____
_____
_____
_____
_____
_____
_____
_____
_____
_____
_____
_____
_____
_____
_____
_____
_____
_____
_____
_____
_____
_____
_____
_____
_____
_____
_____

Morning

1. Mindfulness Exercise

Take a few moments to go through one of the brief mindfulness exercises provided at the beginning of the Journal. Today follow Morning Exercise E.

2. Gratitude

List one thing you are grateful for today. Think of something new from yesterday.

_____

_____

_____

3. Reaffirm your resolution from last night's journal. Write it here.

_____

_____

_____

4. Daily Goal

Write down a practical skill that can help you work toward your resolution today.

_____

_____

_____

5. Writing Exercise

Write for two minutes on anything.

_____

_____

_____

_____

_____

_____

Evening

1. Mindfulness Exercise

Take a moment to go through the brief evening mindfulness exercise provided at the beginning of the Journal.

2. Reflect on Your Day

What went well today? How did you develop or improve (even in small ways) on the specific virtue or skill you're working on this week?

_____

_____

_____

What one or two things do you think need further work in order to develop this virtue or skill?

_____

_____

_____

What specific situations/circumstances are these shortcomings related to?

_____

_____

_____

3. Resolution

Write down what you're going to work on tomorrow to continue to develop your specific skill for this week. Consider doing something that specifically relates to overcoming the challenges you experienced today.

_____

_____

_____

_____

_____

_____

Quote of the Day:

"One can aim at honor both as one ought, and more than one ought, and less than one ought. He whose craving for honor is excessive is said to be ambitious, and he who is deficient in this respect unambitious; while he who seeks honor just as he ought is called great-souled."

— Aristotle

Week 3 (Day 20), Date: ___/___/20__

<u>Morning</u>

1. Mindfulness Exercise

Take a few moments to go through one of the brief mindfulness exercises provided at the beginning of the Journal. Today follow Morning Exercise F.

2. Gratitude

List one thing you are grateful for today. Think of something new from yesterday.

_____
_____
_____

3. Reaffirm your resolution from last night's journal. Write it here.

_____
_____
_____

4. Daily Goal

Write down a practical skill that can help you work toward your resolution today.

_____
_____
_____

5. Writing Exercise

Write for two minutes on anything.

_____
_____
_____
_____
_____
_____

<u>Evening</u>

1. Mindfulness Exercise

Take a moment to go through the brief evening mindfulness exercise provided at the beginning of the Journal.

2. Reflect on Your Day

What went well today? How did you develop or improve (even in small ways) on the specific virtue or skill you're working on this week?

_____

_____

_____

What one or two things do you think need further work in order to develop this virtue or skill?

_____

_____

_____

What specific situations/circumstances are these shortcomings related to?

_____

_____

_____

3. Resolution

Write down what you're going to work on tomorrow to continue to develop your specific skill for this week. Consider doing something that specifically relates to overcoming the challenges you experienced today.

_____

_____

_____

_____

_____

_____

Quote of the Day:

"The offender needs pity, not wrath; those who must needs be corrected, should be treated with tact and gentleness; and one must be always ready to learn better. The best kind of revenge is not to become like them."

— Marcus Aurelius

Way to Go! Keep up the great work!

Let's check in! You have been journaling in your journal perhaps a few days or maybe for many, many weeks. Either way it is good to check in with yourself to keep on track. Journaling consistently morning and evening is a surprisingly challenging commitment, even when the reward of personal growth is felt. Perhaps it's the process of being vulnerable, the change in routine, or the uncertainty or even fear of obtaining personal growth. Take a moment now to think about what, if anything, is getting in your way of daily journaling and how to overcome these roadblocks. If journaling is going well, take a moment to write down what is working and what keeps you on track.

Taking the time to do your journal can help you achieve and maintain personal growth and development. However, you must be willing to risk learning more about yourself and perhaps even feeling uncomfortable as you make changes. This is important to remember; change can be uncomfortable because it is unfamiliar and takes time to become part of a habit. It requires acceptance and willingness. If you are struggling with motivation and making changes, are there areas of yourself that you need to accept and work on willingness to change? If so, how are you going to choose acceptance and willingness?

_____

_____

_____

_____

_____

_____

_____

_____

_____

_____

_____

_____

_____

_____

These questions may be tough to answer. The goal is to provide space to show compassion to yourself if you are struggling and also to encourage you to find ways to push through the challenges as you keep on the path you started so you can reach your goals. Keep it up!

A Special Note: If you're proud of the progress you've been making and want to continue the journey, now is a good time to order your next volume of the _Daily Structured Journal_. Place your order right now to ensure a seamless transition into the next stage of your journey to a better you.

Morning

1. Mindfulness Exercise

Take a few moments to go through one of the brief mindfulness exercises provided at the beginning of the Journal. Today follow Morning Exercise G.

2. Gratitude

List one thing you are grateful for today. Think of something new from yesterday.

_____

_____

_____

3. Reaffirm your resolution from last night's journal. Write it here.

_____

_____

_____

4. Daily Goal

Write down a practical skill that can help you work toward your resolution today.

_____

_____

_____

5. Writing Exercise

Write for two minutes on anything.

_____

_____

_____

_____

_____

_____

<u>Evening</u>

1. Mindfulness Exercise

Take a moment to go through the brief evening mindfulness exercise provided at the beginning of the Journal.

2. Reflect on Your Day

What went well today? How did you develop or improve (even in small ways) on the specific virtue or skill you're working on this week?

_____

_____

_____

What one or two things do you think need further work in order to develop this virtue or skill?

_____

_____

_____

What specific situations/circumstances are these shortcomings related to?

_____

_____

_____

3. Resolution

Write down what you're going to work on tomorrow to continue to develop your specific skill for this week. Consider doing something that specifically relates to overcoming the challenges you experienced today.

_____

_____

_____

_____

_____

_____

_____

Quote of the Day:

"Do not waste what remains of your life in speculating about your neighbors, unless with a view to some mutual benefit. To wonder what so-and-so is doing and why, or what he is saying, or thinking, or scheming – in a word, anything that distracts you from fidelity to the Ruler within you – means a loss of opportunity for some other task."

— Marcus Aurelius

_____
_____
_____
_____
_____
_____
_____
_____
_____
_____
_____
_____
_____
_____
_____
_____
_____
_____
_____
_____
_____
_____
_____
_____
_____

<u>Weekly Check-In</u>

1. Review

Take a moment to reflect on the past week, looking over your notes, and noticing any patterns or trends.

2. Gains

Look at the progress you've made toward your goal over the past week. Write a short summary of your progress here.

_____
_____
_____
_____
_____
_____
_____

3. Ongoing Struggles

Summarize the areas in need of continued growth, and identify the skill or virtue necessary to succeed. Write a brief summary here.

_____
_____
_____
_____
_____
_____
_____

4. Looking Ahead

Give yourself a moment to look over the next seven days. Are there any particular challenges or unique circumstances that you foresee might need special attention? What concrete steps can you plan to take in order to handle these events as best you can? Write these here.

_____

_____

_____

_____

_____

5. Goals

Set a concrete, actionable goal for improving this week. Write your goal here.

_____

_____

_____

_____

_____

6. Planning Positive Experiences

What is one thing you can do to care for yourself this week?

_____

_____

_____

_____

_____

Morning

1. Mindfulness Exercise

Take a few moments to go through one of the brief mindfulness exercises provided at the beginning of the Journal. Today follow Morning Exercise A.

2. Gratitude

List one thing you are grateful for today. Think of something new from yesterday.

_____

_____

_____

3. Reaffirm your resolution from last night's journal. Write it here.

_____

_____

_____

4. Daily Goal

Write down a practical skill that can help you work toward your resolution today.

_____

_____

_____

5. Writing Exercise

Write for two minutes on anything.

_____

_____

_____

_____

_____

_____

Evening

1. Mindfulness Exercise

Take a moment to go through the brief evening mindfulness exercise provided at the beginning of the Journal.

2. Reflect on Your Day

What went well today? How did you develop or improve (even in small ways) on the specific virtue or skill you're working on this week?

_____

_____

_____

What one or two things do you think need further work in order to develop this virtue or skill?

_____

_____

_____

What specific situations/circumstances are these shortcomings related to?

_____

_____

_____

3. Resolution

Write down what you're going to work on tomorrow to continue to develop your specific skill for this week. Consider doing something that specifically relates to overcoming the challenges you experienced today.

_____

_____

_____

_____

_____

_____

Quote of the Day:

"A good grape-picker, who eats the ripe grapes, will not start gathering unripe ones. A charitable and sensible mind takes careful note of whatever virtues it sees in anyone, but a fool looks for faults and defects. And of such it is said: 'They have searched out iniquity and expired in the search.' Do not condemn, even if you see with your eyes, for they are often deceived."

— John Climacus

Week 4 (Day 23), Date: ___/___/20__

<u>Morning</u>

1. Mindfulness Exercise

Take a few moments to go through one of the brief mindfulness exercises provided at the beginning of the Journal. Today follow Morning Exercise B.

2. Gratitude

List one thing you are grateful for today. Think of something new from yesterday.

_____

_____

_____

3. Reaffirm your resolution from last night's journal. Write it here.

_____

_____

_____

4. Daily Goal

Write down a practical skill that can help you work toward your resolution today.

_____

_____

_____

5. Writing Exercise

Write for two minutes on anything.

_____

_____

_____

_____

_____

_____

Evening

1. Mindfulness Exercise

Take a moment to go through the brief evening mindfulness exercise provided at the beginning of the Journal.

2. Reflect on Your Day

What went well today? How did you develop or improve (even in small ways) on the specific virtue or skill you're working on this week?

_____

_____

_____

What one or two things do you think need further work in order to develop this virtue or skill?

_____

_____

_____

What specific situations/circumstances are these shortcomings related to?

_____

_____

_____

3. Resolution

Write down what you're going to work on tomorrow to continue to develop your specific skill for this week. Consider doing something that specifically relates to overcoming the challenges you experienced today.

_____

_____

_____

_____

_____

_____

Quote of the Day:

"Whether we think, speak or act in a good or an evil manner depends upon whether we cling inwardly to virtue or vice."

— Thalassios of Libya

<u>Morning</u>

1. Mindfulness Exercise

Take a few moments to go through one of the brief mindfulness exercises provided at the beginning of the Journal. Today follow Morning Exercise C.

2. Gratitude

List one thing you are grateful for today. Think of something new from yesterday.

_____

_____

_____

3. Reaffirm your resolution from last night's journal. Write it here.

_____

_____

_____

4. Daily Goal

Write down a practical skill that can help you work toward your resolution today.

_____

_____

_____

5. Writing Exercise

Write for two minutes on anything.

_____

_____

_____

_____

_____

_____

Evening

1. Mindfulness Exercise

Take a moment to go through the brief evening mindfulness exercise provided at the beginning of the Journal.

2. Reflect on Your Day

What went well today? How did you develop or improve (even in small ways) on the specific virtue or skill you're working on this week?

_____

_____

_____

What one or two things do you think need further work in order to develop this virtue or skill?

_____

_____

_____

What specific situations/circumstances are these shortcomings related to?

_____

_____

_____

3. Resolution

Write down what you're going to work on tomorrow to continue to develop your specific skill for this week. Consider doing something that specifically relates to overcoming the challenges you experienced today.

_____

_____

_____

_____

_____

_____

Quote of the Day:

"The man who moves a mountain begins by carrying away small stones."

— Confucius

Week 4 (Day 25), Date: __/__/20__

Morning

1. Mindfulness Exercise

Take a few moments to go through one of the brief mindfulness exercises provided at the beginning of the Journal. Today follow Morning Exercise D.

2. Gratitude

List one thing you are grateful for today. Think of something new from yesterday.

_____

_____

_____

3. Reaffirm your resolution from last night's journal. Write it here.

_____

_____

_____

4. Daily Goal

Write down a practical skill that can help you work toward your resolution today.

_____

_____

_____

5. Writing Exercise

Write for two minutes on anything.

_____

_____

_____

_____

_____

Evening

1. Mindfulness Exercise

Take a moment to go through the brief evening mindfulness exercise provided at the beginning of the Journal.

2. Reflect on Your Day

What went well today? How did you develop or improve (even in small ways) on the specific virtue or skill you're working on this week?

_____

_____

_____

What one or two things do you think need further work in order to develop this virtue or skill?

_____

_____

_____

What specific situations/circumstances are these shortcomings related to?

_____

_____

_____

3. Resolution

Write down what you're going to work on tomorrow to continue to develop your specific skill for this week. Consider doing something that specifically relates to overcoming the challenges you experienced today.

_____

_____

_____

_____

_____

_____

Quote of the Day:

"All too soon you will have no more time. You have but one life. Do not stake you happiness on the approval or disapproval of others."

— Marcus Aurelius

Morning

1. Mindfulness Exercise

Take a few moments to go through one of the brief mindfulness exercises provided at the beginning of the Journal. Today follow Morning Exercise E.

2. Gratitude

List one thing you are grateful for today. Think of something new from yesterday.

_____

_____

_____

3. Reaffirm your resolution from last night's journal. Write it here.

_____

_____

_____

4. Daily Goal

Write down a practical skill that can help you work toward your resolution today.

_____

_____

_____

5. Writing Exercise

Write for two minutes on anything.

_____

_____

_____

_____

_____

Evening

1. Mindfulness Exercise

Take a moment to go through the brief evening mindfulness exercise provided at the beginning of the Journal.

2. Reflect on Your Day

What went well today? How did you develop or improve (even in small ways) on the specific virtue or skill you're working on this week?

_____

_____

_____

What one or two things do you think need further work in order to develop this virtue or skill?

_____

_____

_____

What specific situations/circumstances are these shortcomings related to?

_____

_____

_____

3. Resolution

Write down what you're going to work on tomorrow to continue to develop your specific skill for this week. Consider doing something that specifically relates to overcoming the challenges you experienced today.

_____

_____

_____

_____

_____

_____

Quote of the Day:

"Begin each day aware of and prepared for trials and offenses to be committed against yourself; these are due to the offenders' ignorance of what is good or evil. Remember, the good is noble, evil is base, and the culprit is my brother, who has reason and a share of the divine. None of these things can injure me, for no-one can implicate me in what is degrading. I cannot be angry with my brother. Irritation and aversion are obstructions of the natural law."

— Marcus Aurelius

Morning

1. Mindfulness Exercise

Take a few moments to go through one of the brief mindfulness exercises provided at the beginning of the Journal. Today follow Morning Exercise F.

2. Gratitude

List one thing you are grateful for today. Think of something new from yesterday.

_____

_____

_____

3. Reaffirm your resolution from last night's journal. Write it here.

_____

_____

_____

4. Daily Goal

Write down a practical skill that can help you work toward your resolution today.

_____

_____

_____

5. Writing Exercise

Write for two minutes on anything.

_____

_____

_____

_____

_____

_____

Evening

1. Mindfulness Exercise

Take a moment to go through the brief evening mindfulness exercise provided at the beginning of the Journal.

2. Reflect on Your Day

What went well today? How did you develop or improve (even in small ways) on the specific virtue or skill you're working on this week?

_____
_____
_____

What one or two things do you think need further work in order to develop this virtue or skill?

_____
_____
_____

What specific situations/circumstances are these shortcomings related to?

_____
_____
_____

3. Resolution
Write down what you're going to work on tomorrow to continue to develop your specific skill for this week. Consider doing something that specifically relates to overcoming the challenges you experienced today.

_____
_____
_____
_____
_____
_____
_____

Quote of the Day:

"Conquer evil men by your gentle kindness, and make zealous men wonder at your goodness. Put the lover of legality to shame by your compassion. With the afflicted be afflicted in spirit. Love all men."
— Isaac of Syria

<u>Morning</u>

1. Mindfulness Exercise

Take a few moments to go through one of the brief mindfulness exercises provided at the beginning of the Journal. Today follow Morning Exercise G.

2. Gratitude

List one thing you are grateful for today. Think of something new from yesterday.

_____

_____

_____

3. Reaffirm your resolution from last night's journal. Write it here.

_____

_____

_____

4. Daily Goal

Write down a practical skill that can help you work toward your resolution today.

_____

_____

_____

5. Writing Exercise

Write for two minutes on anything.

_____

_____

_____

_____

_____

_____

Evening

1. Mindfulness Exercise

Take a moment to go through the brief evening mindfulness exercise provided at the beginning of the Journal.

2. Reflect on Your Day

What went well today? How did you develop or improve (even in small ways) on the specific virtue or skill you're working on this week?

_____

_____

_____

What one or two things do you think need further work in order to develop this virtue or skill?

_____

_____

_____

What specific situations/circumstances are these shortcomings related to?

_____

_____

_____

3. Resolution

Write down what you're going to work on tomorrow to continue to develop your specific skill for this week. Consider doing something that specifically relates to overcoming the challenges you experienced today.

_____

_____

_____

_____

_____

_____

Quote of the Day:

"Your thoughts at every moment should be simple and kindly, as becomes a social creature (such as you are). Such a person, determined here and now to aspire to the heights, is indeed a priest and minister of the divine, welcoming wholeheartedly whatever falls to his or her lot and rarely wondering what others may be saying, thinking, or doing, except when the common good requires it. Making sure your actions are honorable, and convinced that what befalls you is for the best — such a person does not forget the brotherhood of all rational beings, nor that a concern for everyone is proper to humanity, and they do not follow the world's opinions, but only the opinion of those whose lives accord with true human nature."

— Marcus Aurelius

Weekly Check-In

1. Review

Take a moment to reflect on the past week, looking over your notes, and noticing any patterns or trends.

2. Gains

Look at the progress you've made toward your goal over the past week. Write a short summary of your progress here.

_____

_____

_____

_____

_____

_____

_____

3. Ongoing Struggles

Summarize the areas in need of continued growth, and identify the skill or virtue necessary to succeed. Write a brief summary here.

_____

_____

_____

_____

_____

_____

_____

4. Looking Ahead

Give yourself a moment to look over the next seven days. Are there any particular challenges or unique circumstances that you foresee might need special attention? What concrete steps can you plan to take in order to handle these events as best you can? Write these here.

_____

_____

_____

_____

_____

5. Goals

Set a concrete, actionable goal for improving this week. Write your goal here.

_____

_____

_____

_____

_____

6. Planning Positive Experiences

What is one thing you can do to care for yourself this week?

_____

_____

_____

_____

_____

Morning

1. Mindfulness Exercise

Take a few moments to go through one of the brief mindfulness exercises provided at the beginning of the Journal. Today follow Morning Exercise A.

2. Gratitude

List one thing you are grateful for today. Think of something new from yesterday.

_____

_____

_____

3. Reaffirm your resolution from last night's journal. Write it here.

_____

_____

_____

4. Daily Goal

Write down a practical skill that can help you work toward your resolution today.

_____

_____

_____

5. Writing Exercise

Write for two minutes on anything.

_____

_____

_____

_____

_____

_____

Evening

1. Mindfulness Exercise

Take a moment to go through the brief evening mindfulness exercise provided at the beginning of the Journal.

2. Reflect on Your Day

What went well today? How did you develop or improve (even in small ways) on the specific virtue or skill you're working on this week?

_____

_____

_____

What one or two things do you think need further work in order to develop this virtue or skill?

_____

_____

_____

What specific situations/circumstances are these shortcomings related to?

_____

_____

_____

3. Resolution

Write down what you're going to work on tomorrow to continue to develop your specific skill for this week. Consider doing something that specifically relates to overcoming the challenges you experienced today.

_____

_____

_____

_____

_____

_____

Quote of the Day:

"Patient endurance kills the despair that kills the soul; it teaches the soul to take comfort and not to grow listless in the face of its many battles and afflictions."

-Peter of Damaskos

<u>Morning</u>

1. Mindfulness Exercise

Take a few moments to go through one of the brief mindfulness exercises provided at the beginning of the Journal. Today follow Morning Exercise B.

2. Gratitude

List one thing you are grateful for today. Think of something new from yesterday.

_____

_____

_____

3. Reaffirm your resolution from last night's journal. Write it here.

_____

_____

_____

4. Daily Goal

Write down a practical skill that can help you work toward your resolution today.

_____

_____

_____

5. Writing Exercise

Write for two minutes on anything.

_____

_____

_____

_____

_____

_____

<u>Evening</u>

1. Mindfulness Exercise

Take a moment to go through the brief evening mindfulness exercise provided at the beginning of the Journal.

2. Reflect on Your Day

What went well today? How did you develop or improve (even in small ways) on the specific virtue or skill you're working on this week?

_____

_____

_____

What one or two things do you think need further work in order to develop this virtue or skill?

_____

_____

_____

What specific situations/circumstances are these shortcomings related to?

_____

_____

_____

3. Resolution

Write down what you're going to work on tomorrow to continue to develop your specific skill for this week. Consider doing something that specifically relates to overcoming the challenges you experienced today.

_____

_____

_____

_____

_____

_____

_____

Quote of the Day:

"If you rebuke someone and do it with anger, you have allowed a passion to control you. You have not saved anyone and have destroyed yourself."

— Abba Macarius the Great

Way to Go! Keep up the great work!

Let's check in! You have been journaling in your journal perhaps a few short weeks or maybe for many months. Either way it is good to check in with yourself to keep on track. Journaling consistently morning and evening is a surprisingly challenging commitment, even when the reward of personal growth is felt. Perhaps it's the process of being vulnerable, the change in routine, or the uncertainty or even fear of obtaining personal growth. Take a moment now to think about what, if anything, is getting in your way of daily journaling and how to overcome these roadblocks. If journaling is going well, take a moment to write down what is working and what keeps you on track.

_____

_____

_____

_____

_____

_____

_____

_____

_____

_____

_____

_____

_____

_____

_____

_____

_____

_____

_____

_____

_____

_____

Taking the time to do your journal can help you achieve and maintain personal growth and development. However, you must be willing to risk learning more about yourself and perhaps even feeling uncomfortable as you make changes. This is important to remember; change can be uncomfortable because it is unfamiliar and takes time to become part of a habit. It requires acceptance and willingness. If you are struggling with motivation and making changes, are there areas of yourself that you need to accept and work on willingness to change? If so, how are you going to choose acceptance and willingness?

_____

_____

_____

_____

_____

_____

_____

_____

_____

_____

_____

_____

_____

_____

_____

_____

A Final Note: These questions may be tough to answer. The goal is to provide space to show compassion to yourself if you are struggling and also to encourage you to find ways to push through the challenges as you keep on the path you started so you can reach your goals. Keep it up!

What a long way you've come!

Welcome to the completion of 30 days towards a better you! We hope you enjoyed this journal, but more importantly we hope you used it to do something awesome – become a better you.

If you like what you found inside, encountered any difficulties along the way, or if there is anything we can do to improve your experience next time, we would love to hear from you. Tell us about your journey at **hello@dailystructuredjournal.com**.

We look forward to seeing you again in your next copy of your
Daily Structured Journal!

Order further copies of the *Daily Structured Journal* at
http://dailystructuredjournal.com.